Healthy Eating Habits

by Beth Bence Reinke, MS, RD

BUMBA BOOKS™

LERNER PUBLICATIONS ◆ MINNEAPOLIS

Note to Educators:

Throughout this book, you'll find critical thinking questions. These can be used to engage young readers in thinking critically about the topic and in using the text and photos to do so.

Lerner Publications Company
A division of Lerner Publishing Group, Inc.
241 First Avenue North
Minneapolis, MN 55401 USA

For reading levels and more information, look up this title at www.lernerbooks.com.

Library of Congress Cataloging–in–Publication Data

Names: Reinke, Beth Bence, author.
Title: Healthy eating habits / Beth Bence Reinke, MS, RD.
Description: Minneapolis : Lerner Publications, [2018] | Series: Bumba books. Nutrition matters | Audience: Ages 4–7. | Audience: K to grade 3. | Includes bibliographical references and index.
Identifiers: LCCN 2017049359 (print) | LCCN 2017057863 (ebook) | ISBN 9781541507715 (eb pdf) | ISBN 9781541503427 (lb : alk. paper) | ISBN 9781541526808 (pb : alk. paper)
Subjects: LCSH: Nutrition—Juvenile literature. | Food habits—Juvenile literature. | Health—Juvenile literature.
Classification: LCC TX355 (ebook) | LCC TX355 .R4495 2018 (print) | DDC 613.2—dc23

LC record available at https://lccn.loc.gov/2017049359

Manufactured in the United States of America
1 – CG – 7/15/18

Table of Contents

Healthy Foods

Healthy foods give you energy.

They help you grow.

Do you have healthy eating habits?

A healthy meal has food from every food group.

This is a balanced meal.

Can you name any of the food groups?

Make half the plate fruits

and vegetables.

Put protein and grains

on the other half.

Drink water or milk with your meals.

Fruit juice is OK sometimes.

Eating too much added sugar

is not healthy.

Candy is one food with added sugar.

We should not eat candy often.

What do you like to eat instead of candy?

Fats are part of some foods.

Nuts and seeds have healthy fats.

Olive oil is a healthy fat.

It adds flavor to other foods.

Choose snacks from all the food groups.

Have two or three healthy snacks each day.

When do you eat snacks?

Eating healthy snacks is a

good habit.

What is your favorite

healthy snack?

USDA MyPlate Diagram

This picture shows how much of each food group to eat at meals.

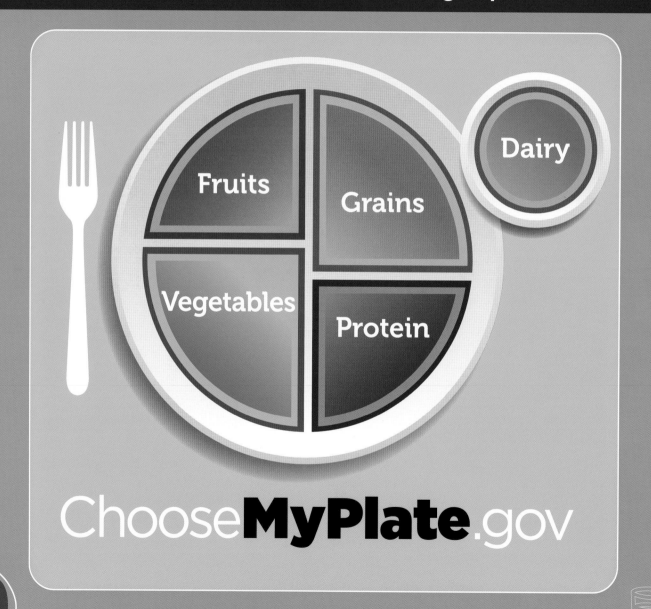

Fruits

Grains

Vegetables

Protein

Dairy

ChooseMyPlate.gov

Picture Glossary

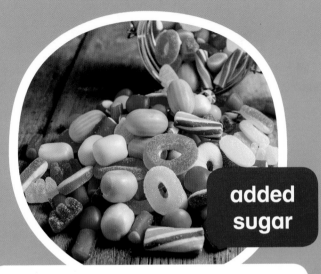

added sugar

sugar that is put into foods

balanced meal

a meal that contains all the food groups

habits

things you do every day

snacks

small amounts of food eaten between meals

Read More

Bellisario, Gina. *Choose Good Food! My Eating Tips*. Minneapolis: Millbrook Press, 2014.

Gleisner, Jenna Lee. *My Body Needs Food*. Mankato, MN: Amicus High Interest, 2015.

Tieck, Sarah. *Eat Well*. Minneapolis: Abdo, 2012.

Index

Photo Credits